NATIONAL GEOGRAPHIC

T0045517

# Big Red Tomatoes

Pamela Graham

Big red tomatoes are smooth and round and juicy.

# tomatoes

They taste good in a salad.

They taste good in a sandwich.

They taste good in a sauce.

Where do tomatoes come from?
They are grown on farms.

They are grown from seeds.

Farmers put the tomato seeds into pots of soil.

Soon, the seeds sprout.
Tiny leaves push up through the soil.

The little tomato plants are called seedlings.

The seedlings grow into plants.
Farmers plant the tomato plants in long rows on their farms.

Water and sunshine
help the plants grow.
Little yellow flowers start to grow
among the leaves.

flower

A tiny tomato forms
in the middle of the flower.

At first the tomato is green.

It grows bigger
and bigger.
Then, as it ripens,
it turns red.

People pick the tomatoes.

The tomatoes are packed
into boxes.
Then they are sent
to markets.

People buy big red tomatoes.

They mix them in a salad.

They eat them in a sandwich.

They cook them
in a sauce.

# Index

farms ..... 6, 11
flowers..... 12, 14
leaves..... 9, 12
markets..... 20
salad ..... 4, 22
sandwich..... 4, 22
sauce..... 5, 23
seedlings..... 10, 11
seeds..... 7, 8, 9
soil ..... 8, 9